What If God Took a Holiday?

A Positive Prayer & Activity Book For The Whole Family

What If God Took A Holiday? - A Positive Prayer & Activity Book For The Whole Family
Written by Anita Sechesky
Copyright © 2020 by LWL PUBLISHING HOUSE
A division of Anita Sechesky – Living Without Limitations Inc.

All rights reserved. No part of this publication may be reproduced, distributed or transmitted in any form or by any means, including photocopying, recording, or other electronic or mechanical methods, without prior written permission of the publisher, except in the case of brief quotations embodied in critical reviews and certain other non-commercial uses permitted by copyright law. For permission requests, write to the publisher, addressed "Attention: Permissions Coordinator," at the address below.

Anita Sechesky – Living Without Limitations Inc.
lwlclienthelp@gmail.com
www.lwlpublishinghouse.com

Book Layout © 2020 LWL PUBLISHING HOUSE
What If God Took A Holiday? - A Positive Prayer & Activity Book For The Whole Family

Anita Sechesky – Living Without Limitations Inc.
ISBN 978-1-988867-59-5

Book Cover: N. Sechesky
Inside Layout: N. Sechesky & LWL PUBLISHING HOUSE

Dedication

This book is dedicated to anyone and everyone who has ever prayed a simple prayer of help to God.

It is my greatest desire that we can all remember that God is always available for each one of us, even though we often forget about Him.

Anita Sechesky

The Lord's Prayer

Our Father in heaven,
may your name be kept holy.
May your Kingdom come soon.
May your will be done on earth,
as it is in heaven.

Give us today the food we need,
and forgive us our sins,
as we have forgiven those who sin against
us. And don't let us yield to temptation,
but rescue us from the evil one.

Amen.

Matthew 6:9-13 (NLT) New Living Translation

DEAR GOD; THANK YOU FOR ALWAYS BEING THERE AND SENDING YOUR GUARDIAN ANGEL TO WATCH OVER ME. I PRAY THAT YOUR PEACE WILL SURROUND ME WITH THE SWEETEST DREAMS EVER. AMEN.

DEAR GOD; THANK YOU FOR SENDING YOUR ONLY SON JESUS, WHO GAVE HIS LIFE FOR ME SO THAT I CAN BE HEALED.
I ACCEPT JESUS INTO MY LIFE WITH ALL OF HEAVEN'S BLESSINGS SURROUNDING ME AND I PRAY FOR MY FRIENDS AND FAMILY SO THEY CAN BE HEALED TOO.
AMEN.

DEAR GOD; THANK YOU FOR NEVER TAKING A HOLIDAY EVEN THOUGH YOU CREATED A DAY OF REST FOR ALL OF US TO TAKE CARE OF OURSELVES.
YOU ALWAYS KNOW WHAT'S BEST FOR EACH ONE OF US.
AMEN.

Activity Section

DOT - TO - DOT

1.wombat 2.echidna 3.koala 4.duckbill 5.kangaroo 6.kiwi 7.alligator 8.nambat 9.parrot 10.bat

1.alpaca 2.armadillo 3.parrot 4.iguana 5.sloth 6.anteater 7.tapir 8.turtle 9.toucan 10.snake

1.eagle 2.raccoon 3.porcupine 4.bear 5.armadillo 6.reindeer 7.crocodile 8.tapir 9.lynx 10.elk 11.wolf

FIND 5 DIFFERENCES

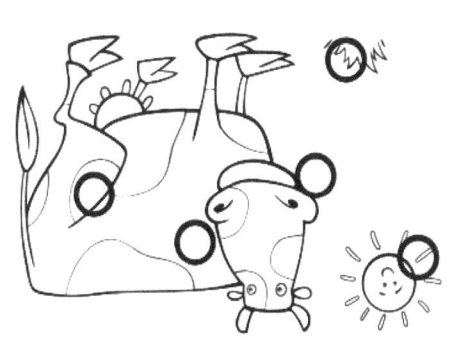

FIND **10** DIFFERENCES

FIND 10 DIFFERENCES

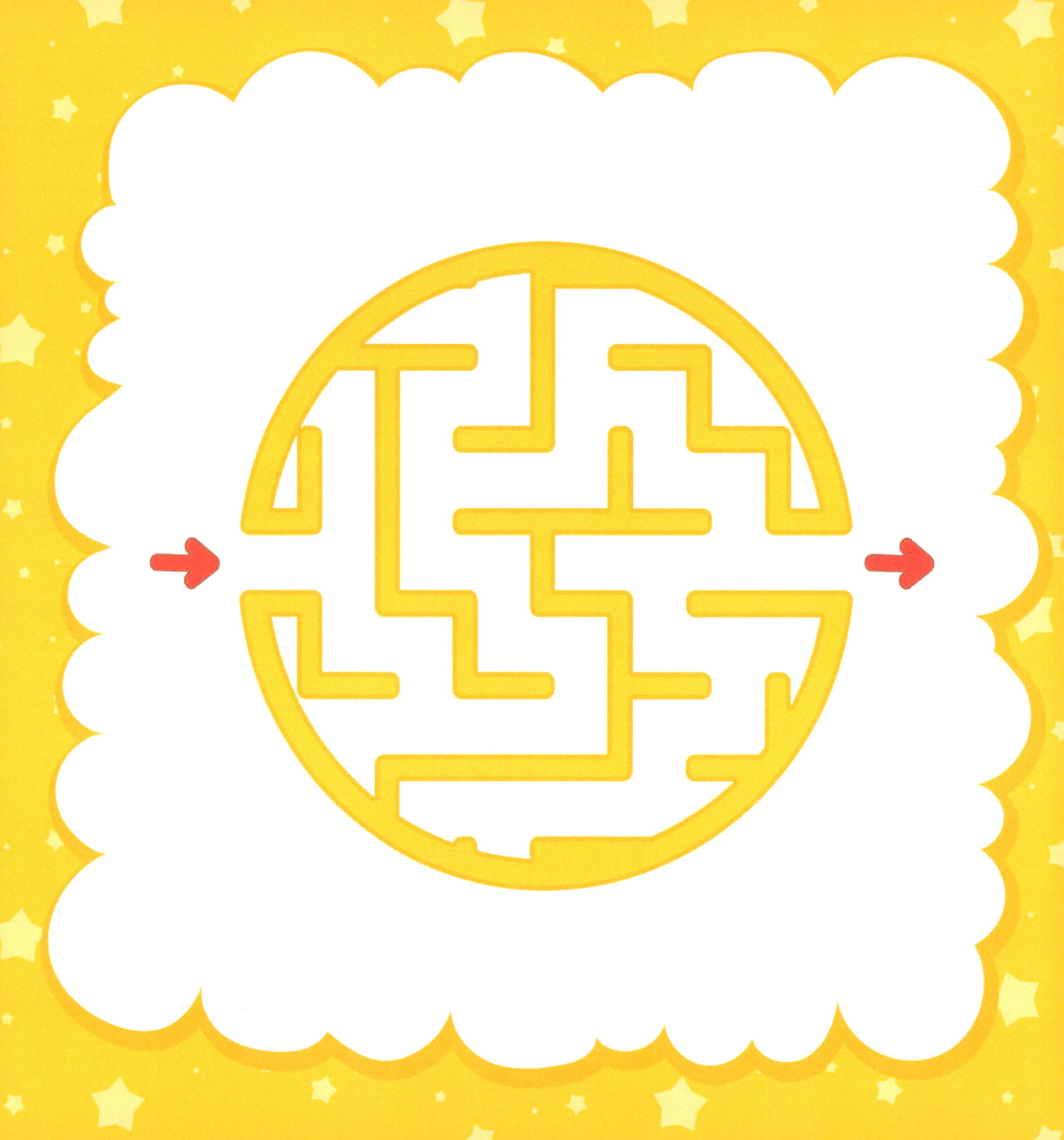

FIND
7
DIFFERENCES

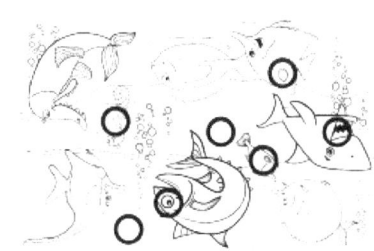

Psalm 91

Those who live in the shelter of the Most High
will find rest in the shadow of the Almighty.

This I declare about the Lord:
He alone is my refuge, my place of safety;
he is my God, and I trust him.
For he will rescue you from every trap
and protect you from deadly disease.
He will cover you with his feathers.
He will shelter you with his wings.
His faithful promises are your armor and
protection.

Do not be afraid of the terrors of the night, nor
the arrow that flies in the day.
Do not dread the disease that stalks in darkness,
nor the disaster that strikes at midday.

Though a thousand fall at your side,
though ten thousand are dying around you, these
evils will not touch you.
Just open your eyes,
and see how the wicked are punished.

If you make the Lord your refuge,
if you make the Most High your shelter,
no evil will conquer you;
no plague will come near your home.
For he will order his angels
to protect you wherever you go.
They will hold you up with their hands
so you won't even hurt your foot on a stone.
You will trample upon lions and cobras;
you will crush fierce lions and serpents under your feet!

The Lord says, "I will rescue those who love me.
I will protect those who trust in my name.
When they call on me, I will answer;
I will be with them in trouble.
I will rescue and honor them.
I will reward them with a long life
and give them my salvation."

Amen.

Psalm 91:1-16 (NLT) New Living Translation

BONUS PAGES FROM...

Living Without Limitations COURAGE
My First Reflective Journal & Activity Book 1

Written by Anita Sechesky

STRONG

It takes a STRONG person to look past the things that made you sad.

I AM STRONG because I can overcome sadness!

GOOD

It takes a GOOD person to be kind to anyone who hurt them.

I AM GOOD because I am kind to everyone!

FORGIVE

It takes a special kind of person to FORGIVE those who don't like you.

I am special because I FORGIVE everyone!

SUPER

It takes a SUPER person to be better than the people who hurt you.

I AM SUPER because no one can hurt me!

With Love & Gratitude

Special Thanks of Appreciation to God,
my Heavenly Father, Provider and Protector.
It is because of you that I can do all things.
May everything I do always be pleasing to you.

My children, Nathaniel & Sammy - You are both my Joy and Inspirations. Thank you for your fresh perspectives.
My husband, Stephen - Thank you for your loving support and dedication to see this project to completion.
My parents, Jean & Jetty Seergobin - I am so blessed to be your child. Thank you for your unfailing love, support and guidance.
My Brother, Trevor Seergobin - Thank you for your encouragement.
My Mom-in-Law - Thank you for your love and your son, I'm so blessed to have you both in my life.

LWL Media Support Team - You are the best! Thank you for your patience in perfecting this AWESOME book.

A EXTRA SPECIAL thanks to Nathaniel Sechesky for the design layout and to all my former patients, nursing colleagues, clients, family & friends - Each of you have inspired the vision for this book during the world pandemic.

About The Author

Anita is an RN, ICF-Certified Professional Coach, and Motivational Keynote Speaker. She is the Owner/Founder and CEO of LWL PUBLISHING HOUSE, and will have successfully published approximately 500+ authors by the end of 2020. Anita is also a wife and the mother of two boys, the author & Visionary of multiple Best-Selling books in the Inspirational, Self-Healing, and Faith genres.

It is her greatest desire that she can promote healing of not only the body, but also the mind and spirit of each man, woman, and child through her vision for LWL PUBLISHING HOUSE. Anita facilitates *Inspired to Write* workshops, Masterclasses on Emotional Healing, and speaks at events that focus on living your best life possible without emotional limitations.

She has worked in many health care facilities and Emergency Rooms in Southwestern Ontario and has witnessed the breakdown of emotional health, relationships, and family dynamics when dealing with trauma or a crisis.

If you would like to have Anita speak at your event or organization, or if you are interested in writing your own inspired story and would like to work with Anita to help you bring your best efforts forward to publication, please contact her below.

Lastly, if you are interested in joining one of our anthologies in the works that you can share your short story in, please visit our website for more details.

Website: www.lwlpublishinghouse.com
Email: lwlclienthelp@gmail.com

Listen to Anita's INSPIRED TO WRITE Podcast:
https://www.spreaker.com/user/anitasechesky

Anita Sechesky RN, ICF-CPC
#1 Best-Selling Author, Founder, CEO and Publisher at LWL PUBLISHING HOUSE

www.ingramcontent.com/pod-product-compliance
Lightning Source LLC
LaVergne TN
LVHW072112070426
835510LV00002B/22